Postcards from a City Ablaze

A Poetry Collection

By David Greshel

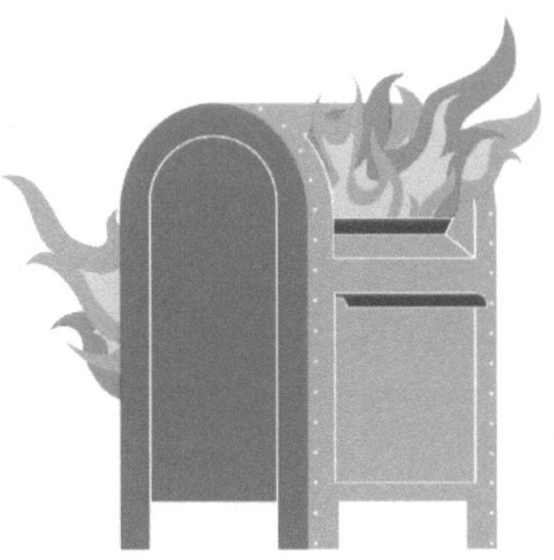

Original Mailbox Icon art by Steve Zmijewski

Introduction

Well, here we are once again. Another collection, another introduction. In my heart of hearts, I always want to believe I have something amazing and profound to say here to lead you into the poetry that fills the following pages. I want to be able to tell you about all of the blood I shed to bring these pieces to life, all the emotions I had to experience in order to draw myself out in tiny doses and breathe a unique life into each one. I want to regale you with amazing tales of guts spilled in earnest across three years of writing to the rhythm of an internal metronome that never seems to skip a beat. I want to embody the mythic frame of a poet I saw once in a dream and have heard whispered about in the pages of history; strange characters that capture the imagination of the general public in ways that only make sense in the clarity of hindsight.

I want to do all of those things…but being totally honest I'm a pretty regular guy that just happens be somewhat adept at stringing words and phrases together in a manner that some find engaging and thought provoking. Plus, it still happens to be a cathartic bit of processing that I've learned to be okay with sharing. It occasionally involves a bit of verbal bloodshed and something not unlike an exorcism, but the end result is only slightly dramatic.

Postcards from a City Ablaze is something I actually suggested as a subtitle for another project. That idea was shot down, but I liked it enough that I decided it was the perfect title for this new book. I'm still somewhat amazed that this is the fourth collection of poetry that I'm releasing out into the wild. I'm drawn back to the thought of releasing my first collection back in 2012, when I wondered if anyone would truly be interested in what I've created. I've grown a lot in the 8 years since, and the pieces that make up this volume include some of the very best that I've written to date.

I'm truly grateful for those that have supported me along this journey as an author, and I hope you find enjoyment in the pages that follow. I hope that, even if poetry isn't really your thing, there's something within these pages that speaks to you in previously unimagined ways. Who knows, maybe next time I'll finally find the time to collect all the stories tumbling around in my head and finally put them down on paper…maybe the next book will finally be a more long-form experience.

But for now…see you where the sidewalk ends…

Dave
August 2020

Acknowledgements

There is so much that goes into bringing a book to life, and this one is no different. As an independent publisher with a current staff of one, I wear a great many hats during this process. That does not mean, however, that there aren't plenty of other people that lend their talents and support along the way.

Thank you to the many wonderful and talented writers in the Instagram poetry community for the encouragement and constructive critique. You are invaluable to the process and most often the first to see new material as it unfolds.

Thank you to my friends and family, who have been the biggest encouragement across four volumes - I love you all so much.

Thank you to God the creator - through whom all things have been made and for the gift of your Son.

Extra special thanks to the following people who helped bring this volume to life through the Kickstarter community:

Travis Gibb
Jonathan Hedrick
Michael Tremarche
Kehinde Umar
Jemlynn Tatlonghari
Amy Graft
Heidi Hess
Laura Purdie
Chris Cox
Chuck Pineau
Donna Middleton
Joel Gonzalez
Aubra Brown
Kimberle Williams
Roni Pavick
Troy Stewart
Rick Shea
Jackie Noto
ML
Rachel Mintz
Ken Cohen
Debbie Oliveras
Debra Lobin
Rachel Carroll
Mick Davis
Liz Lugo
Justin Chaffiot
Marc Collette

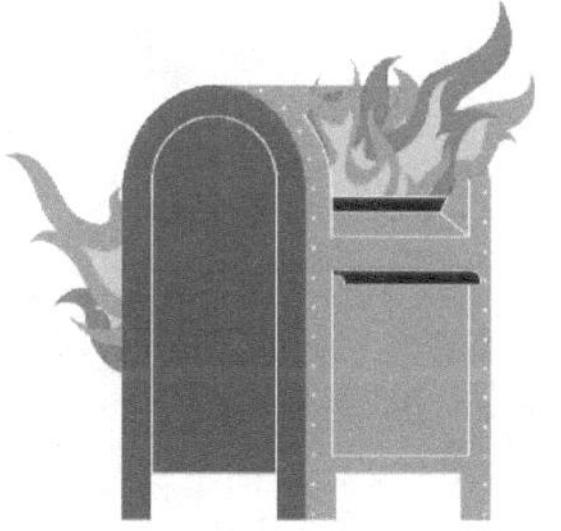

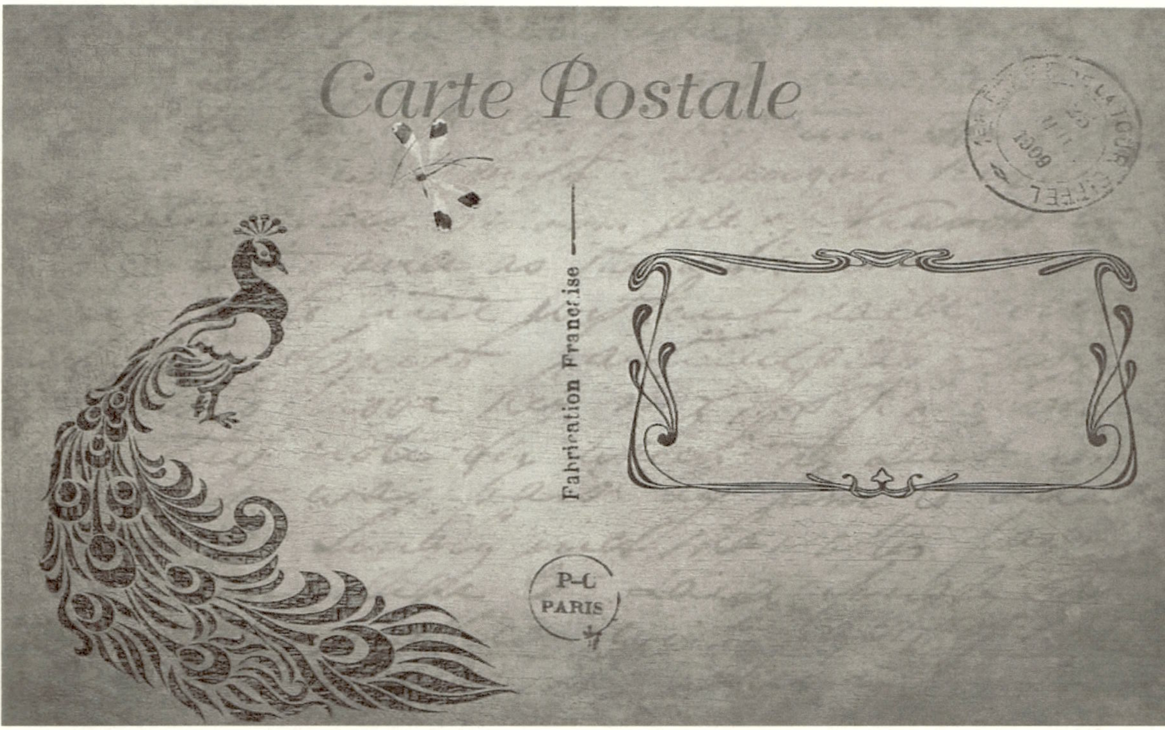
Carte Postale
Fabrication Française
P-C
PARIS

Prometheus Regrets, Sisyphus Forgets

I was a fire breather held in legend
Igniting southern countryside
With naught but a careless whisper
Feigning levity and idle desire
While bathing in immolation
That spreads with every uttered syllable
Dancing off the tongue
In clever idioms and hollow platitudes
That pretend to offer righteous fury
And leave nothing but dust and ashes
In their wake

I am the raging inferno you embrace
The self-damning prophecy
You claim as infallible directive

I am the undeniable blaze
And there is no space safe
From this misguided malaise

Pink Scribbles on Paper Tablecloths

Skies alive in starlight
Falling in satellite daydreams
Wishing for stolen ideas
Taking flight in secret
Pushing past broken limits
Bleeding through the speed of sound
In the last temptation
Aboard the silver shadow
Bound for all points beyond
Not a moment past perfection
Still anticipating the endless journey

Crossfire Hurricanes and their Aftermath

Darkness rolled in
Fresh on the heels of an onrushing storm
Barreling down the east Florida coast
Leaving a swathe of detritus in the wake

Calm and serene
A collective sigh of relief
Exhaled in unison
Floating from the breath of tired survivors
Seeking only refuge in escape

Dawn shatters the slate skyline
Sending streaming shafts of liquid amber
Into the humid atmosphere
Igniting the daylight that never dies
And the hope that never goes out

Searching for the Beautiful Among the Tombs of Purple Skies and Amber Waves

There's a mystery out there worth solving
Whatever happened to my America?
She got lost somewhere back when
Buried beneath the weight of history
And all the party crashing ideals
Never fully realized or considered
Overwritten in the blood of secrecy
Meant only to advance the status quo
Hidden in the guise of patriotic vitriol
And exuding empty promises of change
While smothering the light of hope
In partisan political games

Whatever happened to my America?
She's still out there
Huddled with the tired masses
Broken and abused
By those who claimed to love her
But with a spirit far from extinguished
And a fire just waiting to blaze
Under God with true liberty
And justice for all

<u>Maybe I'm not Fine, but Would You Know?</u>

The walls in this room
Have heard every secret
Listened to all the confessions
Whispered on August nights
Reflected all the subtle lies
Believed in September's onslaught
Absorbed all the errant tears
Burning down well-worn tracks
On flush cheeks
That preface another October breakfast

Choke it all down
Paint the façade
Smile at everyone

"I'm fine."

Conversations with Myself Before Coffee

In the quiet morning hours
Well before the appearance of dawn
And the waking dream of light
I sit in the arms of contemplation
Nursing a steaming shot of vitality
And wondering what we mean by forever
When we have no proof of concept
For something that has no end
Infinity if you will
A leap of faith

I don't know much about forever
But when I find you I won't let go
Until my last breath is gone

We'll leave forever to the divine

<u>Rip Van Winkle's Retirement Plan in Full Effect</u>

Quietly creative in the morning shade
Spinning stories for water lily sprites
And laughing with the chipmunks
Chittering in the oaken boughs overhead
Scurrying after autumn acorns
Bound for the winter stockade

Eyes closed in the rest of arboreal arms
Listening to the cheerful birdsong
Fluttering between the branches
Calling out to their brethren in flight
Leaving homes behind
In favor of warmer southern shores

Heartbeat slowly diminishing
Mimicking the approaching hibernation
Creeping upon this shedding forest
Tumbling into an ancient slumber cycle

Let me sleep with my natural kin
Wake me in the dawn of centennial spring

AM Self-Psychiatry via Keystroke

We're all stumbling around like survivors in the fallout…or dreaming wide awake…unsure of the things we cling to as our reality and wondering if…at any second…it might all slip away like the fading echo of some perfect melody we only half heard in the moonlight…these anxious thoughts crowd my memories and overwhelm any desires I might think to have…until they're all projected onto you and I'm left to puzzle out why no one ever seems to measure up while the silhouette of my reflection smirks in silent disbelief…and the self-inflicted delusions roam around free…

...But What Do I Know Anyway...

Promising solutions disappear
Evaporating in the rising heat of contention
And the suffocating stench of opinion
Founded on nothing but misplaced feelings
And uncontested emotions
That leave this heart a slave
To the whims and demands
Of an ignorant vox populi
More concerned with their own fleeting happiness
To ever give a momentary thought
To the notion that they've been blinded
By the very things they crave
And the vultures circling overhead
Are the servants of their idols
Just waiting to pick their carcasses clean

Unknown Funeral at Sea

The cold seeped in through tiny cracks
Spreading out from shallow foundations
While we searched the horizons
For the fabled lands of freedom
And the wellsprings of opportunity
That filled storied pages
And fueled fever dreams
Worth risking everything for

Sunlight cracks the fading darkness
Illuminating these foreign shores
Encased in steel barricades
Barbed wire welcome mats
No vacancies to be found
Only hornets and hand grenades
And an iron lady liberty
Now banished beneath the sea

We were the tired and poor
The huddled masses once welcomed
Chasing safety and asylum
Now finding closed fists
Not open hands
We died here in the harbor
Drowning amid the sounds of cheering
Bleeding out from all the greatness

They're all Last Words When You're Always on Fire

A flash of incendiary emotion sparks
A runaway conflagration that swallows
All this forested logic and reason
Turning ancient understanding to ashes
On the altar of hysteria
Unwilling to be contained or subdued
Sacrificing any would be moderation
On the burning stakes of popular opinion
Leaving behind nothing
But the smell of napalm and charcoal

Time Capsule Thoughts in a Vacuum

I reached into the dying light of the sun and knew it for what it was…the end of everything that once held us…the last gasp of ordinary afternoons…close your eyes and see me how I used to be and I'll smile and remember you for who you'll someday become…ascend into the blooming nightfall and ride on the back of the starchild…gazing out into the galaxy we imagined yet never will contain us…and just know the dream is never over…

Awakened from a Self-Delusion

I climbed the golden heights alone
Basking in the warmth of Spring
Unfolding beneath the clearest skies
And found the silence strange
Despite rebirth wildly abounding

Amidst all the urban cacophony
That invades my daily existence
Have I forgotten the natural symphony?

Have the countless hours
Wrapped in concrete and steel
Enraptured in our own handiwork
Completely dulled my senses?

Standing on the cliff's edge
Overlooking the verdant valley
All thoughts slip quietly away
Awestruck by this majesty on display

Good News in the Midst of an Oncoming Storm

There wasn't supposed to be a light
No dancing flame or shining sun
No radiating glow or lunar reflection
Nothing but the swollen pride of death
And the insatiable hunger of the grave

Darkness
It seemed
Had finally won

...and there was night...and then morning...the third day...

It started out so subtly
Nearly imperceptibly
Tempo rising to a thundering roar
Striking fear in the hearts of Roman watchmen
As the tombstone failed to remain
And rolled aside

There wasn't supposed to be a light
But He would not be contained
And we knew now it was far from over
Guided by this light that never goes out
And the newfound hope in resurrection

Excised and Under the Microscope of Introspection

It's often a dragging knife's edge
The clarity of hindsight
Exposing all the ragged wounds
Still dripping in the wreckage
Of what was once a friendship
Now spread for examination
Beneath the coroner's unforgiving light
That searches out the truth of the demise
Without an ounce of compassion
Or any telltale sign of remorse

DOA was hardly a surprising outcome
We were walking corpses
Long before the ship disappeared
Beneath the surface
Without a trace of innocence
Or a back missing a blade

The curtain has been called
Nothing left for us here
But the song of a phantom
And the promise of forgotten graves

Building a Case for Pyrotechnics

There were moments that passed in solitude
Pensive, expansive in their reflection
And hinting at the languid pace of eternity
Settling over the hills like an evening fog
Permeating the atmosphere

It was then that I learned to stop and breathe
To release the shackled tensions
And let go of the tortured rage held captive
Self-made prisoner realizing he holds the keys
Walking into the light without shame

They were moments
Disappearing blips on the radar
In an undiscovered countryside
And a dream worth chasing
The fabled peace in our time

Living in the Space between You and Forever

Stranger dreams unfold at length
Riding the swell of the even tide
Afloat on the collective hopes of a tired nation
Gasping for shallow breaths
In the crashing surf
Trying to remain upright
Amidst the oncoming waves

It felt alive and electric
Climbing up onto the beach
Laying there panting
While the water races outlines
Angels in the sand

A welcome warmth spreads through
Radiating through exhausted limbs
Dripping dry in the disappearing sun
As an anthem sighs
A body unwinds
And unravels in a slow decline
Waiting for the recoil
In the ever open arms of nightfall

Searching for Meaning in Temples for Dogs and Gardens of Sound

We discovered life beyond the wheel
And took a chance on love in a mind riot
Without a second thought given pause
Even in the midst of black days
And blacker rain
Refusing to be outshined by memories
Of slaves and bulldozers en masse
And recovering lost artifacts
Buried on the fourth of July
That recall forgotten birth rituals
And an inevitable hunger strike

We never really thought it might be over soon
An ending just like suicide
And a falling blackhole sun
You were the highway
And now our euphoria morning
With a hope to carry on

Say hello to Heaven for us
And reach down every once in awhile
We'll be here braving this room
A thousand years wide
Drinking holy water
And searching for that all night thing

Living in the Aftermath of a Disco Inferno

What did it all mean to you?
When there was nothing to hide behind
No veil to mask the machinations
Of a misbegotten wizard
Or the misdirection of a streetwalking charlatan

When all the world was laid completely bare
Naked in the unforgiving sunlight
Burning away every last vestige of pretense
What were the thoughts that captured your mind?

Did you even think at all?

Because the stake is completely ablaze
And my flesh is beginning to melt
But even there amidst the screams of the dying
And the seething hatred of the zealots
I find myself incapable of escaping a singular thought

What did it all mean to you?

Pleading with Better Angels on Holiday

We make all these bold proclamations
Grand statements with dramatic exposition
Predicated on an idealistic notion
Of some higher evolution unfolding within
And yet the evidence of our advancement
Is strangely undefined
Or even completely absent

We somehow still revel in destruction
With dreams of malice and malignant intent
Aimed at anyone we deem unworthy
Or guilty of the crime of difference
We're the same killers we've always been
Enraptured by annihilation
And exhaling this callous disease

Hear these words in earnest
Not as fatalistic cynicism
More like empirical observation
And an undying challenge
We were built for more than this
We can truly rise up out of these depths
Burn so bright even the stars need shade

Shadows on the Styx

Tendrils of silver smoke
Spiral skyward
Stretching in supplication
Towards ethereal spirits
That roam these haunting hours
She walks along this mortal plane
Completely unhindered by convention
And radiating sultry confidence
Attracting undeserving acolytes
Looking to bathe in the flames of desire
Finding only the ice of disdain
She simply laughs and fades out
Disappearing in the waning twilight
Fabled princess of midnight

Typewritten Odometer Readings

It sort of hung there in the Summer air
A favorite refrain
Lingering on your salty tongue
And cutting through this swollen night
All that sass dripping like morphine
Wrapped in that vocal melody
Sliding past your quivering lips
With every ounce of conviction mustered

I memorized every word
Wound it back again…and again
Rinse and repeat
A last long goodnight
Goodbye

It's not a tune on my radio these days

It's like Forever only Backwards

Seems like we're always at that part
Where the record skips
Unable to hear the entirety
Stuck on an unintended groove
That captures only the dying strains
Of a moody piano chord
Lost in the crackle and pop
Like every conversation we never had
Or mistaken for tears in a thunderstorm
That wouldn't be noticed
Missing in minor keys
We are the underwhelming ghosts
Of all these half-imagined dreams
Walk on past without concern
We're only bleeding in step and time
Last request on the hotline
Giving you all the nothing
You could ever need

Flashes of Brilliance in an Eclipse

There was darkness here…which is a lot like saying it's wet in the water…but there was darkness that covered the landscape and it was comfortable and familiar…even sort of safe in a weird aspect but it wasn't satisfying…something just kept me restless…roaming…always roaming…and a tiny flicker caught my eye off in the distance…almost imperceptible…but I had to know…had to see this strange phenomenon that pulled e ever closer…shimmering flame suspended in a beckoning…stinging the eyes with a blinding bright…curiosity compels me to reach out…fingers closing around the fiery tongue…to extinguish?...no, to capture…to feel the warmth…and it burned…oh, it burned…set me ablaze…but I could finally see…and hope was alive…so alive…enveloping me in an embrace I never want to leave…

Fire Eaters and Lazy Dreamers

I wanted all the warmth of the light
Without the cost of the cleansing burn
As if there was no work involved
In the art of growth
Just wake up one morning at the highest point
With no time ever paid to the climb
...that's how it works right?

I wanted to feel the radiant heat of midday
While firmly planted in the kingdom of midnight
Pretending dual citizenship
is attainable and encouraged
While the itch of conscience tickles my soul
And offers only definitive choice
One path or the other
So very Robert Frost

I want all the rewards of a life well lived
Still learning to count the cost of getting there
Still learning to trust the burn

Racing Dragons on Sea Tides

Fading away out in the distance
Last vestige of the familiar escaping
To the backside of the horizon
As we set our course into the unknown
Gilded in wild lights and darkest blues
That echo the former life of a shadow
Caught too long in the fireplace
And more accustomed to the steady heat
Than the icy tendrils of an alien nightfall
Where I hold on to the dreams of you
Dancing in the summer sun
Stolen kisses in a feather rain
And all the whispered promises
Of young lovers eloping one afternoon
Without a single thought given
To reactionary surprise
More real than midnight fantasy
And we tumble off the edge of the map
To court sirens and devils on the open sea
Stretching the very heart of me
While I yearn for nothing more than contact
And the fireplace at your bedside

Something About Inquiring Minds and Knowledge Out of Reach

The ink is fading on these pages
Yellowed and curling with ages past
Gathering dust alongside
Countless forgotten tomes
In this library of the lost
And I wonder if those words
Will forever go unread
Doomed to a history of silence
Will we ever know the heart
Of these hidden philosophies
And does he ever get the girl?

Pictogram Couplets Under Glass

Listening for the solar frequency
Orbiting within primordial airwaves
Emitting subliminal pulses
That slither into aural orifices
And whisper tempting appetites
In storied languages long deceased
And vanished from the pages of memory
Leaving me all of the clever words
And a loaded melody
With only an empty hall to sing to
And a lonely moon to romance
In the arms of a pregnant night

The Truth and Other Things You aren't Prepared to Handle

Pressed for absolute answers
To the vaguest of questions
Spun from a tangled inquiry
Only half conceived
And not at all prepared
For the knowledge now bestowed

Poetry is an exorcism
Inwardly directed
Self-inflicted
And the power of the pen
Compels these demons
Out onto the empty page

Knots, Tongues, and Other Ties in Action

Deep breaths and anxious thoughts
Crowding and crowing for attention
With every step inching closer down the aisle
And a future filled with unknown hours
Primed to unfold and bloom
With a guiding love in play

Still, I Do is akin to jumping off a cliff
With no measure of the depths below
Or time to dwell on imaginary scenarios
And learning you both can fly

It's a future being built in the moments you share
The flames you kindle
With every one a stretching root of life
Supporting this newly blossomed family tree

Romantic Chemical Alterations and the Carnival in Between

Skyfaring sojourners silently swing
Circling the azure expanse
Searching for signs of solitude
Spread out among the fading headstones
Still dreaming of suburbia

We sung the dirge
Read last rites
Mourned the inevitable passing
Long before these phantoms
Found their new identity
At the head of this black parade

It All Smells The Same No Matter What You Call It

Screams and sirens fill the soundscapes
Mixed with the staccato pounding
Of blood rushing headlong
As eyes go wide in utter disbelief
At the horror unfolding unwinding
In the guise of ideology
Old as the hands of time themselves

Paint it any shade you fancy
Supremacist
Nationalist
Antifa
The -ists go on and on
Revealing myriad angles
Of this shared picture

You're the bastard children of Cain
Breathing murder in every word uttered
Killing your siblings in selfish indignation
Clinging to impotent violence
Choking on dry mouthed rage

There is no place for you here
You have been marked
And it's time for you to wander on

The Gift of Air from My Lungs

I just wanted to exhale
Release this breath too long suspended
Caught between the crawling seconds
I felt your eyes discovering every secret
Laid bare in the smoldering gaze
Igniting unspoken desires deferred

Deflating lungs and escaping air
Signal the break-neck return
Of time's unrelenting passage
And the dissolution of an undeniable moment
Destined to be analyzed ad infinitum

In the midst of awakened epiphany
One thought rings with clarity
In the unfolding knowledge
That upon our awaiting encounter
I might not ever breathe again

First Class Ticket to the Twilight Epiphany

Closed my eyes and drifted out to sea
Intergalactic hitchhiker floating past
Lazily cresting celestial waves
Listening as the last strains of 'I Keep a Diary'
Fade out and fall away
Mingling with the dust and detritus
Streaking in passing comet tails
Shifting currents and solar flares
Bleeding the atmospheric edge
Plummeting towards a crimson landscape
Existence flashing through firebrands
Memory film on repeat
Burning in the wreckage
Resurrected in the rising steam
Last dream of a Martian sunrise
Last rites of a life left behind

...and this is why emotions are untrustworthy...

I never really knew what I wanted
If we're truly being honest
Walked through our entire existence
In the kind of haze held in reserve
For the sort of oddly desperate
Or eagerly blinded

So…yeah
It wasn't even a bit surprising
The day you finally walked out
With a look that eviscerated my defenses
Trailing the sadness of 'might've been'
And an echo of footsteps I'll not forget

Never wanted you more than that moment
Clarity ever late to the party
Dragging honesty in tow
It's clear I didn't love you
Not in any way that made sense
And I don't know if I'm relieved or devastated

Playing Twister in a Hurricane

There's a heaviness in the air
Suspended in the morass of uncertainty
And oozing with anxiety
Choking on the aftertaste of fear

Shades of paranoia
Paint by number propaganda
Color every page in outrage
Designer product placement
On the heels of an oncoming apocalypse

If you're confused
You're not alone
It just means you're paying attention
And this nonsense
Simply does not compute

Somewhere in Between a Wing and a Prayer

Found myself alive at the strangest time
High on the prospect of optimism
Surprised by the strength of an identity
Only evident in the most recent of memories
And I wonder if all this newfound joy
Was always one of the possibilities
If I could have sheltered here
Throughout the raging storms

It's funny in a way
The things we allow ourselves to really see
When we pull back from the immediate
And focus on the mural as a whole
Not the errant brushstroke anxiety

Round Pegs and Square Holes

Not really sure where the disconnect
Interrupted the train of thought
En route to the station of intent
Or which part of the idea of freedom
Is lost in the sea of ancillary static
That echoes in waves of feedback
From this current paradigm
Radiating from your reflection

There is no release in this approach
Hugging the paint by numbers confines
And the imagined safety
Of this predetermined bubble and box
We're not shaped in cookie cutter sets
Or preselected outputs
And there's no room for 'one size fits all'

It's not out of malice or devious design
But well meaning isn't synonymous with being right
We're not asked to present the prettiest picture
Or an unblemished life

We're asked to follow
And to love
And that might look a bit different on everyone
No need to pass your list around
Or announce your place on the path
Just be salt and light
And trust that everyone is making their way

Their part of the path just might have a different view

Carte Postale

mi amore

tu me manques

Fabrication Française

P-C
PARIS

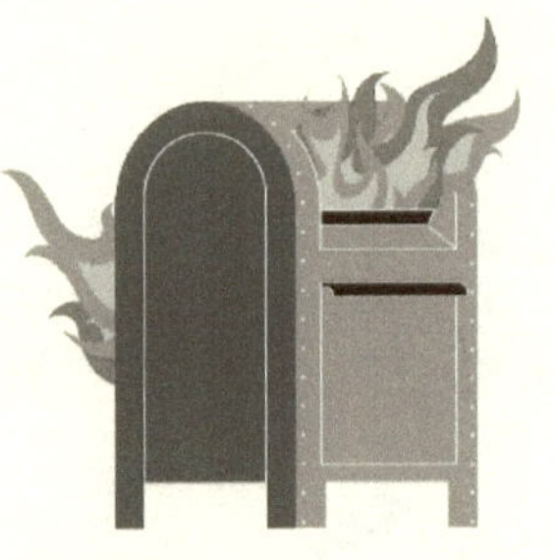

Souls and Seeds Emerging

It spun out of an overwhelming darkness
Tiny pricks of light foreign to the obsidian sleep
Interrupting the familiar doldrums
And beckoning towards the wild unknown

Enter the house of change
First class flight to a knock out
And a dreaded catalyst unannounced
Leaving the whole of self-perception shattered
Echoing the fading strains of requiem

Change breeds choice
Floundering fetal forebear
Destiny driven deliverance
Each one enticing with epiphany
Imagined or otherwise

Embrace the moment
Feel the scales fall from new eyes
And the decayed flesh peel away
As we are reborn from seeds of defiant hope
Revealing Kingdom creatures
And sojourning saints
Awakened to the flames of resistance
Setting fire to funeral rags
And breathing in the intoxicating incense
Of an undeniably true identity

The Fluidity of Self-Perception

Just a thought
The span of a moment
A breath on my lips
And a glimmer on the horizon
Past the realm of rational
Borderline fantastical

Merely a flash
Unworthy of a mention
Or the external attention
But I lived a dozen lifetimes
In that ephemeral glance

Rewriting roadmaps
Marked in scars and regrets
Reimagining stolen dreams
Lost to degenerate cynics
Resurrecting destinies
Executed by jealous idols

I left the world
Followed an internal intuition
Bathed in blood and fire
Found a light beyond
Returning now with thunderous revelation

Don't blink

I Have No Words...and That's Part of the Problem

She asked me what it felt like
To drown on dry land
As if the experience was one
She might want to take for a spin

Might be a morbid curiosity
Fatalistic dance with destiny
Or a razorbladed truth willingly unseen

Didn't notice the faded scars
Still masked in plastic happiness
Or hear the unspoken pleas
Floating beneath strained laughter

Floodgates finally torn asunder
Unleashing torrential enlightenment

What's it like to drown?
Cause all this evidence is suffocating
Yet somehow the circumstances
Are still open to debate

Still sorting out
Just how many open wounds it took
Before I finally saw you bleed...

Burning in the Desert Winds

Guess I should've known this time
When you wandered off
Into the smoldering evening
That it was more than just momentary
And a far cry from the ordinary

Can't remember all the words released
Or the ones we left unspoken
Less of an argument
Than a sorrowful realization
Resigned to take the sunset curtain call
Before the inevitable decline

Stranded in the impending collapse
Or so it might appear
But if you someday change your mind
You'll not find me orphaned here
Play one last sad song
To all we ever were
And meet me on the gleaming shores
Of second chances and mended bridges
In the glittering brilliance
Of one more tequila sunrise

Burning Brighter than a Simple Memorial Flame

I tend to dread the hollow echo
Of the ticking second hand
Knowing what awaits in the hours ahead
At the turn of a calendar page

Doesn't matter really
Just how long it's been
Tears the wound open every time
Remembering you've left and gone

So many things I want to tell you
All the times I wished to share
And all I said I would trade
For just one more day

Time is a healer
Though not always obvious
Opting to build beautiful memories
To alleviate these ragged scars

It's never any easier
Never been the same
But I know you're forever with me
Alive in the love we bear

Redirecting Stolen Spotlights

There's really no account for willingness
In the midst of lessons learned
And I'd say most were acquired
At the expense of blood and inner turmoil
Agonizing over imagined psychosis

Still the knowledge hits like crashing cymbals
Awakening from dreams of naivete

I am not your savior
No matter how hard I might try to be
No matter the purity of every intention
You'll find no salvation
Looking solely at me

Writing our Names in the Milky Way

There was a tantalizing story out there
Nestled among the glowing nebulae
And the supernova southern stars
Birthing infant galaxies
That dream of charming lives
Dwelling in extraterrestrial pursuit
Of embellished tales

Sojourning on streaking comet tails
I read every word etched in heated stone
Followed hidden clues and clever phrases
Sewn into your skin
Tattooed enigmas

I took you in like oxygen
Coveted breath of life in a vacuum
Consumed every line 'til we bled the same
Spilling our shared soliloquy
Across this universe of you and me

You Sang About Seasons Changing

Waning daylight stirs the coming chill
Signaling Autumn's zenith
And the inevitable embrace of Winter
Where I dwell in half-remembered dreams
Suspended in visions of encroaching ice
And a rebirth in virgin snowfall

Fragments

There is that last moment hanging just on the edge of consciousness where we all wonder…"is this it?"…and then tumble into the arms of awaiting slumber…to drift in the waters of the dream and imagine the what ifs and never were…

We are the exploratory exposition of every single moment spent wondering if there was more to it than what we have experienced up until this exact point in our own timeline tracing back to the spot we first thought of anything at all…to think…to dream…to wonder and explore…is the essence of being truly alive…

If this were a Film there would be Sad Music and a Montage

Evening rainfall patters on the rooftop
Liquid rhythm softly echoing in the halls
Where I reflect and roam
Listening for the remnants of conversations
Long past and faded in the interim
Full of empty words and shallow laments

There was never enough to say
Despite the voluminous vocabulary on display
And yet every part of me trembles
At all the thoughts and memories shared
Slowly disappearing like dissipating fog
Leaving only colorless clarity
And a solitary affair

Something about Flights of Fancy

Found myself aimless and afloat
Drifting along fickle currents
Of half-held convictions
That seem to shift in concert
With the pendulum breeze
Of unpopular opinion

We went with the flow
Followed the rising tide
Left our minds so open
Everything unique was swept away
In favor of the hive

It's far easier to be sure
Unburdened by the necessary weight
Of producing thought
But there's still the faintest memory
A fading recollection
Of personal responsibility

Would it Matter if I Told You I Was?

"Are you afraid to die?"

Such a simple question
Pointed…direct…
Piercing hazy layers
Of emotional auto-response
And a shaky defiance
Of the undiscovered unknown
That awaits

"No."

"Are you afraid to live?"

Speculation overdrive
In myriad existential scenarios
Sorted and predisposed
To target shackled inhibitions
Hidden from consideration
And alive in spite of revelation

"No."

"Are you just afraid?"

Sugar Plum Visions and Candy Cane Dreams

Twinkling lights peeking through
Like multicolored fireflies warming Winter haze
In the expanse of indigo and ivory
Here in late December

Heady aromas invade the atmosphere
Douglas fir and gingerbread
Intermingled with Yule log warmth
Smoldering in the well-kept fireplace

Huddled here together
Snuggled beneath this blanket mountain
Hot cocoa kisses and peppermint dreams
And it's easy to believe
If only for tonight
In peace on earth and goodwill to all men

Humpty Dumpty Health Plan Hijinks

Woke up in a haze
Recollecting the sound of sparks
And the acrid smell of smoke
From all the misspent fireworks
Wondering if the scorch marks
crisscrossing the vaulted ceiling
void the initial deposit
or just add a little character
to this borrowed apartment

Revelation seemed within reach
Transfixed in the growth of clarity
But there's no security in a cyclone
No safety in the dragon's breath
And we make our farewells
To the phantoms of gilded dreams
Caught within the fading stories
We build to get us through the night

So much of it feels like an exercise
Practice in the art of dissertation
And colorful sleight of hand
Wandering through cliché responses
Toward a final exaggeration
With all the noble flourish
Of a national obsession

I want to fall to pieces
But I'm afraid of all the best attempts
At putting me back together
In the shadow of the midnight valley

A Difference in Measured Degrees of Introspection

There's an often startling procession
To even the most timid recollections
Spilling out of uncovered omission
Amongst the illustrated composition
And favoring the empty decisions
Idly discussed like something lost
But never quite out of mind

Sifting through the passages
Drifting in ink stained histories
Wrought in fractured perceptions
That split time and reality
Into fading curiosities
Spread out past infinity

Imagination fuels this inquiry
Creating convenient catalysts
From empty points of emphasis
And lights the flame of avarice
While we slice ourselves to pieces

Death by a thousand cuts of absence

Cheat Codes and Easter Eggs

It's in the empty AM hours
Dreamless and catatonic
Interrupted only by the necessity of breath
Where I wonder if this is truly sleep
Or if the program has been paused
Queued at save point convenience
Waiting for an aimless player's interest
In this ramshackle simulation
An approximation of living
In some designer's imagination
But it begs a myriad of questions
Stolen from an existential syllabus
Bent on discovering our undisputed purpose
In the art of conversation
And the nature of violence
As the measure of enlightenment
Of the civilized and savages

Achievement unlocked
An anchor and a cross
Weighed down and crucified
By every anxious nightmare
Every hypothetical thought

Dreamless and catatonic never looked so good

Substance in the Sojourning

Starlight tumbled earthward
Sparking golden wishes
And unnamed hopes
Fanciful sentiments
For a spectrum of rays
Travelling several lifetimes
To expire in a glittering shower
But for a moment's delight
Aloft in the eyes of a child
Whispering innocent prayers
And wondering at the heavens

Were You Remembering Everything I Said or was that Just My Imagination

Thinking it may have lingered just a bit too long
A question framed in verse and rhyme
Punctuating Sunday conversations
Encompassing this flight of dreams
The ones we're left to dream alone
Here among the graves of poets and libertines
Resurrected and walking among the stones
Wondering if this is what I truly thought
I'd find in my heart when you were gone
Knowing I was ever the fool for you
And I just had to let that feeling linger...

It's so cold in Ireland this morning
Heavy in the weight of your absence
Longing for the scent of cranberries
Scattered in the fresh fallen snow

Growth Expounded, Results May Vary

There are subtle things discovered
In the quiet hours
Just before the awakening of dawn
Floating on the cusp of hope
Revelations illuminated
In the comfort of joy

There are flashes of cognition
Born from the flames of tribulation
And the tutelage of loss
Secrets only uncovered
In a shower of blood and regret
On the outset of clarity

Don't forsake the smiles
Or the call of happiness
Because you feel only the bloodshed
Teaches the stronger lessons

Don't avoid the possibility of pain
Or the ache of infliction
In favor of ignorant bliss
Or fear of what might be revealed

<u>This Might Be Showbiz, but You're No P.T. Barnum</u>

Spinning coppers spark debate
Tossed in flippant defiance
Erupting from the end of a megaphone
Leaving little room for civil discourse
In such a public arena
And one might almost believe
That this was your permanent intention
Shouting down any opposition
With a totality of practiced derision
That we've come to expect
From your porcine primadonna acolytes
Made up and utterly obvious
Cue the spectacle
Entrance stage left

...but that's just my two cents
For whatever that gets you these days

Is it Parallel or Multi? I get My Verses Mixed Up

Out in the deepest obsidian expanse
Pricked and bleeding illumination
In the racing starlight spreading in eons
Devoured by the singularity in absence
Everything that ever was or will be
Balanced on the head of a pin
Suspended in infinite possibility

Is this the unfolding scope of reality
Or just another elaborate fantasy?

Smoking Cherry Bombs in Place of Cigarettes

We are enraptured
Entangled

Emblazoned with all the hallmarks
Of enlightened ecstasy
Ensconced in encompassing desires
Held within a fever dream
Imaging calculated explosives
Indoor fireworks in flight
Burning the bed to embers and ashes
Erupting in the aftermath
Of our endless love
Eternally echoing

We are enraptured
Entangled

There was a King Once, Just ask the Queen

It drifted in on the lazy breeze
Hot and sultry hanging heavy
Laid across a pseudo-summer night
Hushed and hallowed on a river bank
Mississippi mud and a fading melody
Echo in the ghosts of Memphis
Recalling music in another life
Still wafting through the airwaves
Bleeding blues and soul
Somewhere near the ragged end of a lonely street
In a hotel famed for shattered hearts
Where we listen to a strained piano
Playing all across the broken pieces
Solidarity in subtle sympathy
Sung in background harmony
Calling for slow dance solitaire
In the memory of midnight

Living in Between the Quick and the Dead

Unaware of eons crawling past
Here outside the bounds
Of something as inconsequential as time
And it's a wonder to survive
Banished and ignored
Left to my own devices
Which are rather minimal
When the only thing
That isn't nothing
Is you

The first sound in millennia
Crackles and thunders
Splitting stars with a whisper
Calling me forth to glorious purpose
In the cleansing fire of absolution
Erasing every name
That was never mine

Romero's Waltz

In my most selfish moments
I long for an Ezekiel to prophesy
And breathe life into these tired bones
Resurrecting all we ever were
For one last dance on the promenade
One last flight amid the constellations

Hindsight abounds in searing waves
Illuminating every stabbing reminder
And all the blood we left behind
In the wake of our verbal assaults
Playful sparring once upon a time
Turned full blown character assassination

Memory leaves me spent and weary
Parading an entourage of fading ghosts
And subtle temptations of 'might've been'
But in the end I'm only dancing
With the rotting corpse of us
And these bones long past their expiration

A Dream I Half Forgot

I remember the melting snow
The slush and puddles receding
Uncovering dormant earth
Awakening from its Winter slumber
And it might've seemed ugly
Muddy, barren, and brown
But it teemed with unseen possibilities
Unfolding in shoots of verdant green
Stabbing skyward
Breaking free

I remember those same echoes
Reverberating through my introspection
And it may have seemed unappealing
But the possibilities are endless
With new life just lying in wait
For the opportune moment to alight

I remember

I remember

Lizard King and a Pin Up Queen

They called it a ghost highway
Stretching out across the western desert
Illuminated by the moon and stars
And those old flickering headlights
Carving up the asphalt
Devoured beneath the beat-up Chevy pickup
Rumbling through the night
On the way to nowhere we might remember
Listening to a reptile monarch croon away
About soul kitchens and backdoor men
Set adrift on crystal ships with LA women

The coyotes howl in the distance
Celebration or lament, who can say?

The engine breathed its last
Stalled out in Death Valley
We wandered further out into nothing
Guided by psychedelic whispers
Waiting for the sun

Envisioning a Kind of Blue in Stereo

We were chasing something ancient
Riding notes of blue in waves
Aloft on sonic chariots
Searching out the uncovered shades
Hiding in the aural atmospheres
Tucked in between the melodies
Phrased in the timing of breaths
Escaping swollen lungs

We saw the unbroken horizon
Crested in the shining illumination
Stretching forth from the union of earth and sea
Imagination speaks in harmony
Weaving scales and symphonies
Invoking strains of a love supreme
And the holy requiem of dreams

Ruminations on Scorched Earth Souls

I fell apart all those years ago
Deconstructed in the aftermath
Scattered like detritus in the wind
Reduced to mere existence
Hollow
Husk

Determination surfaces
Rising in sober reflections
Unwilling to simply fade away
In the absence of your spark

You were a harbinger of chaos
A raging wildfire unbound
Set loose on my inhibitions
And I held on 'til I was ashen
But I'm not quite ready
To return to the dust

Empty Stars on Shredded Clothing

History is enveloped in a haunting
Caught out in a fog of recompense
Called to account for fading ashes
That still cling to the furnace maw
And a sickly sweet gaseous odor
Permeating shower chambers
While fragile human frames wither
Tattooed serial numbers
Erased names

The groaning echoes hang in the halls
Accusing revisionist saboteurs
Screaming across decades
And bleeding darkness in dreams
Raining yellow stars and pink triangles
Six million ghosts crying out
Begging to be remembered

Afloat on the Hope of Memory

I woke with the rising dawn
Laid out on an ochre stretch of beach
Recovering from another hidden night
In the arms of an aloha fantasy
Enraptured and enthralled
In the haze of a dream
Fading in the materializing sun

Wandered down to the waves
Salty foam swirling between sandy toes
Dancing through the essence of Summer
Arriving on the heels of a thunderstorm
And an obsidian Spring
Disappearing on the golden breeze

Color me alive
If just for one moment
Breathe and remember
If only today

Staring Down from the Venusian High Dive

Stepping out onto a precipice
A literal metaphorical edge
Of weighted culmination
Balanced in perfect symmetry
Between a leap of faith
And nothing left to lose
Out here among the shifting tides of imagined galaxies
A veritable universe of options
Designed to tantalize
Paralyze
Snared in the over-thought
Overwrought
All too careful analysis
Keeping everything mundane
And disappointingly predictable

…and that's when you grabbed my hand and
whispered
"just jump"

Co-star in a One Man Show

Speaking in subtle soliloquies
Sheltered in these evening shadows
Breathing solitary lullabies
On enigmatic frequencies
Buried within the white noise
Broadcasting twenty four seven
Across encrypted pirate channels

Is anyone listening?

Solara Gloriana

The sun cracked the horizon
Splintering light a million ways
Just as it always has before
And yet a shadow lingers here
An empty space
A kind of void
Left in the wake of your passing
One I never thought to see so soon

We are brothers in spirit and blood
Might not have always been easy
Might not have always been good
But we had each other
And an unbreakable bond
That runs deeper than rivers of crimson

It doesn't feel real
Can't believe we won't be talking
About our favorite hockey team
Or the next big dream
But I know this is not the end
And it's not the last of us

You're kept within every heartbeat
Alive in the light of love
Cherished in immortal memories
Until my final breath escapes

Sifting Through the Weight of Consequence

The hardest lessons linger
Bouncing through endless imagining
In the expanse of possibility
Begging to be learned and known
In these moments of lucidity

We are all Cain
Bathed in rage and murderous intent
Burning in an inferno of jealousy

We are all Abel
Earnestly seeking righteousness
Broken and bleeding left for dead

We are a sum of choices made
Truths we hold on to
Reactions to consequence

We are a fount of searing potential
Be it angelic or monstrous
The waters are fed from within

Burning Mementos with Soggy Matches

Out here on the fringes of the known
I find myself pushing deeper
Testing the boundaries of mystery
Challenging the monsters off the map
And looking to uncover the wonder
Lost to the minutiae of routine

Not content to live in the pain
Recycling those moments
Like some treasured memory
Or misbegotten identity
No longer will I sing its refrain
Or leave it in a place of power

This is not a denial
I cannot simply forget
Yet neither will I revel in the hurt
Or treat it as a coveted lover

Its effect on the path is clear
I can trace the sunken scars
Like a braille incantation
But I am not my pain
And I refuse to let it define me

Ghosts and Artifacts are Common Here

A sidewinder sleepily shuffles
Sifting through a lonely telegram
A few decades left behind
And wondering whose eyes
Were the last to behold it
Whose tears left these faded stains

I always wanted to find that place
Alive in the lines of a song
Alight on a breeze of melody
Breathing hope and purpose
Between the subtle pauses

Immortal in shining harmony
Immutable in daring profession

The kind of dreams imagined
When every minute bleeds a tale
You'd never be inclined to tell
Much less suffer to endure

New salt stains the yellowed page
Lidless eyes rimmed and reddened
Lamenting a goodbye
Long since surrendered

Presented Without Commentary

Another morning cracks free
Splintering the tired darkness
Beneath a kaleidoscopic dawn
Shifting tendrils stretch and strike
Seducing the swollen egos
Of well-meaning citizenry
Ensnared in marionette strings
To dance at the whim of a puppeteer
Playing at Neo-Machiavellian blues
Driving barbed wire wedges
Between otherwise friends
Now screaming bloody murder
Drawing lines in the sand

No matter how righteous it seems
There are no winners here
We are all deceived

Carte Postale

Fabrication Française

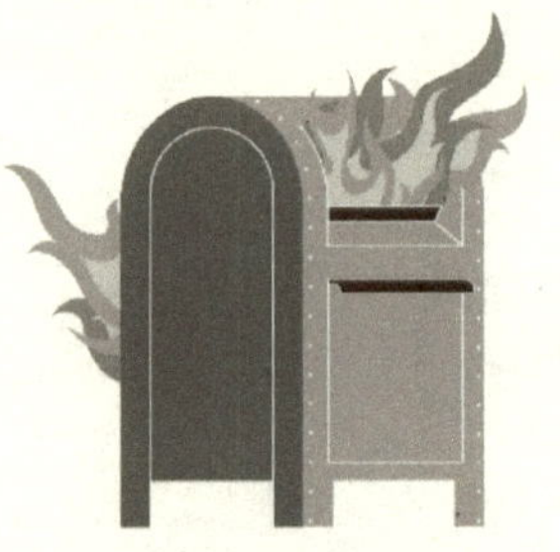

There's a Freeway where a Swing-set was Meant to Be

It's the achingly familiar sounds
That trigger the deepest memories of you
Recalling some minor detail in a fog
That evokes a gentle laugh
And a few quiet tears

Like the creaky stair in the hallway
Third from the top
The one your dad was always going to fix
But never did
You always knew when I came in
No matter how hard I tried not to wake you

They tore that old house down today
It shuddered and groaned
As the dozer cut a path through our kitchen
Where we sat at that antique table
Plotting future endeavors
The frame split and cracked
The foundation breathed a last goodbye
Crumbling beneath weighted tread

And then it was gone
Like all those better tomorrows
We weren't destined to see

The Effort Alone is Maddening

Fade in with the opening lines
Light up the jaded silver matinee
With your close-up monologue
On some imagined glamour scene
Somewhere east of fabled Eden
Where Amazonian beauty is effortless
Mythical and unconcerned

Flash back to reality
Peek behind the curtain
Expose the digital wizard
Manipulating every miniscule detail
'til it all screams perfection

Oh, you pretty things!
So enraptured in the illusion
You thought might make you whole

All that paint serves to cover nothing
Highlighting a broken empty shell

I Did Play One on TV Once

She was there in the sullen aftermath
Recalling melancholic comfort
In the arms of a Summer thunderstorm
Ruminating on the sudden loss
Of an innocent infatuation
Washed out and evaporated
In the sweltering solar flares
Crisscrossing inferno atmospheres
Dreaming of Dr. Strangelove
Or a rocket and a bomb

Anemic Liars and Thieves

We shuffled into view come morning
A shambling ensemble barely alive
In the finest tatters and filth
These local gutters can spare
First class accommodations
From the hard luck haberdashery

We watched them there uptown
Resplendent opulence on display
A petty royalty
Sipping pennyroyal tea
Awash in an illusion of superiority
And inflated self-opinion

There's a single step between us
Yet the chasm seems impossible
And we just love to watch each other fall

Echoes of Apocalypse

The skies yawned and cracked
Hemorrhaging stardust serenades
That bled in sparkling rivers
Beneath the red-hot moon
Calling out to animalistic impulses
Boiling within pulsing veins
Adrenaline instincts on overdrive
With an overwhelming urge to howl
Clawing to the surface of intention
Swinging a fistful of bone and steel
In punctuated polyrhythms
Aiming at a tonality of freedom
And an untethered soul afire

Lead Balloons and their Improbable Flight Plans

I counted every beat and measure
With an actuated mental metronome
Attuned to the secret rhythms
known deep within these earthen bowels
long thought lost to frozen eons

I could hear the rising melody
Cresting the crescendo
With the faintest hints unbound
In the resonating dissonance
Crawling beneath the harmony
Tilting us toward cacophony

The inevitable finale looms
Imbued with a subtle grandeur
Tempting an eternal audience
With our vocal immigrant song
Demanding binaural attention
In a therapeutic primal scream

<u>No Really, We're Much Better Off Now</u>

Pages flip and flicker
Fluttering in the artificial breeze
Finding their rest on calendar days
Anniversaries in August alkali
And all the hate mail you scent
With a lascivious vitriol
And a touch of sage
To remind me it was something good once
In some far off younger day
When we were both too dumb to care
And far too crazy to live

Yet we did

And all the waves of remorse
Crashed our existential crisis
Left us sundered at the seams
With you practicing poison verse
And me carving new glyphs
In what little skin I have left

There's a Story Here that Might Never End

The horizon loomed in the distance
Never creeping closer in the gloom
Yet it beckons with each hour passed
Echoing a fading promise
On a lilting siren song
Spinning seafaring serenades
That fuel these awakened desires
To navigate the nether realms
And brave the blackened firebrands
Amidst the gaping maw of nothing
Tempting discord and despair
At the overwhelming vanity
Of an attempt to reach that place
Where the ocean and the sky connect
And yet that little speck of light
Flickers and shimmers off the waves
And we sail ever on…

The Inferno Behind Door Number 3

It all started with the clever burning
Careful and precise in execution
With every bit of minutiae accounted for
In the pristine pyrotechnic patterns
That crawl through the smoking kindling
And the surrounding acreage ablaze
Collateral damage concisely constructed
To mask the intensive immolation
And herald this unmistakable annihilation

It all started with the clever burning
And I realized far too late
That it was all we might ever be
That you willfully chose to incinerate

Trash or Treasure in Perspective

There was always something
Beautiful about the wreckage
Of another bold attempt
A kind of gleaming golden aura
Where most see only scattered refuse

The resulting twisted carnage
Not wholly unexpected
But a miscalculation all the same
Ninth configuration unchecked
In an ongoing derelict dream

You might see only folly
A looming lunacy unbound
I see a passion unreserved
A sizzling skyrocket in flight
With no surrender in sight

Speaking Forgotten Alien Verse

I wondered why these thoughts
Always seemed to come in August
To punctuate the hot summer nights
With a side of suffocating delirium
And just a pinch of anxious insomnia
And the only thing that ever broke the tension
Was the steady rhythm of your measured breathing
As you slept so peacefully beside me
And I imagined what sort of dreams
Must be dancing through your mind
A land of sunshine alchemy
Stretching out in all directions
With no sense of urgency
Or anywhere in particular to be
And I think that's simply wonderful
A kind of Heaven I'd like to see
If this Hell inside me now
Would just take a hint and leave
But for now I'll take this solace
And just keep watching as you sleep

Cats and Fiddles are on Deck

Evening glistened in the descent
Catching the glittering half-light
That still flickered on the horizon
And called to mind all the memoirs
Of the dying stars now peeking out
And dotting the indigo canopy
That spreads in all directions
While we lie on our backs and stare
Searching for virgin constellations
And wondering whose name they bore
Or why we never made more wishes
For fear the sky might fall
While we laughed at the absurdity
Of cows and spoons clearing the moon
And I would give just about anything
For a few more nights like that
Where you were so close to me
When we were so young and free
When there was nothing like living
When tomorrow didn't matter
Just tonight and right now
Just you and me

Selling a Shared Delusion is a Solo Affair

I thought I might have found a cure

A salve for all the wounds incised
Casually inflicted
Self or otherwise

A balm for all the burning flesh
Cracked and peeling
In shades of reptilian sheds

An elixir for the screaming aches
That travel the body electric
Faster than these pain killers bleed

I thought I might've found it
The magical mystery miracle
To erase these wasted years

Just another mirage in the haze
And there are forty dunes to go

A Story You Might Have Heard Before

We spent the last vestiges of summer
Wrapped in the embrace of swollen heat
And the scent of evening jasmine
With a wish to know the deepest secrets
We never dared to speak aloud together
Never brought into the dimming light
For fear of an unwelcome revelation
And a ceremonial exit

Anxiety unfounded
Born from overactive mental faculties
Bent on overwhelming fragile emotion

Laughter soothes these fraying nerves
Reassurance in your voice
And the subtle brush of your skin
In that moment I am immortal
Breathing in the incense of your eternity

You Think that's Bad; You Should Hear what isn't Said

It's the scent of bloodshed
Thick and immense
Hanging in the poisoned air
That emanates from your person
And broadcasts your mouth for war
In every destructive syllable you utter

'Only' can't Even Begin to Describe It

Startled for the briefest of seconds
Caught up in the ephemeral moment
When our lips collided in mutual hunger
And lingered in the addictive taste
Of a newly shared kiss
That sparks a craving
To know you in the deepest places
And feel it all from the inside
Until nothing separate remains
Fading into me to fade into you
And we breathe in unison
Bleed in uniform singularity
Awakened to the severed hearts
Now mended and pulsing
Screaming this song of new life

The Empty Armory is not a Positive

We often skip over the recollections
Preferring to let that reflection pass
In favor of the more immediate bliss
And the short-term satisfaction
Unleashing the ravenous hounds of war
When diplomacy would better suit
This tactile delegation

Where will it all lead you?
When these Washington bullets
Find unexplainable targets
That echo home
In the worst ways imaginable

When does the lunatic parade end?

Steel Horses and Fake Wanted Posters

This was a dream once
Living in the moments between
Disconnected last minute flights
And one-night extravaganzas
Never to be seen again
This side of the Milky Way
Where we traveled at length
And marked all the sights captured
With creative contraband

Time runs at a constant blur
Where we're never quite sure
If it's Tuesday or last January
But the bus rolls on
The towns and clubs all look the same
While the candle melts to nothing
And tempers fizzle towards explosion

It seems so easy to live like this
The proverbial 'man in a suitcase'
But all I want to see is my cat
My bed
And the far side of hibernation

It All Comes Back Around

Howling voices echoed through the canyons
A lonesome evening song
Reverberating off the ancient stone
In a painted history along the mesa

I lived a hundred lifetimes
Riding the wild breath of the desert highway
Winding along the dwindling river bed
Discovering all those darkened places
Obscured in the gathering storms

The stars danced and fell in waves
Glittering into the ebony expanse
While we watched and wished
And reminisced
Remembering the eons long past
Dreaming of millennia to come

Camelot in Foreclosure

Golden spires erupted in the fading heat
The last striking rays of Summer unseen
In the haste to install an Autumn kingdom
And crown another pretender to the throne
Intent on chaining us to the gristmill
Beasts of burden without recourse
Trudging through the wreckage of limousines
And decaying battlefield carcasses
Remnants of forgotten wars on vanity

Salvation in Stereo

Fleeting thoughts escape into the ether
Released to seek an audible existence
In the unexplored emotional expanse
Opening out onto the relational canvas
Stretched over the gleaming surface
Charred fields of black diamonds
That ripple in the aqua breeze
With a subtle obsidian glint that flares
Catching snowblind eyes thought lost
With a whisper of hope
And a beacon for home

Kitchen Sinks and Everything In Between

Heavy scents hung hollow
Wafting in the waning Summer breeze
Enticing the sweetest surrender
And the promise of unending rapture
In the throes of unearthly delights
That re-ignite this dormant passion
And overwhelm my fragile senses

Little butterfly wings aflutter
Recalling every brush of flesh
Every stolen moonlit kiss
That sanctified our hallowed ground
And unwound this 'all night thing'
Into fever dreams without end

Seasons on the Stereo and Spice Under Glass

That cooler air tumbled down
Rolling out of the ascendant peaks
And signaling the oncoming change
Poised to envelope these hills
In the shrouded spectral comforts
Of Autumn's living end

We stand here silent
Examining the quickened chill
That seeps into exhausted bones
A not so subtle reminder
Of Winter nipping at the heels
And the promise of blessed slumber

Torching the Proverbial Countryside One Encounter at a Time

The darkness stretched out past existence
Roiling and churning through untold eons
Spent stumbling toward awareness
And scathing self-realization

We emerged from the grip of a fever dream
Unfolding in the sliver of amber sunshine
Flickering…beckoning…
Enraptured by the shimmering brilliance
In the company of the burning ones

The flames spiral outward in earnest
Igniting defiant seeds of hopeful change
That spread from heart to heart
Through enlightened minds and open doors
On the wings of unguarded epiphany

Andrews Avenue Allegory

You're never truly prepared
No matter how much you've tried
Prepped and steeled your nerves
Anticipating the inevitability
Of this quiet mortal passing

Wasn't ready for this to be last call
I was hoping for another round of dominoes
Another rummy hand
A slice of caramel spice cake
Or the most amazing pancakes

I already miss the sweetest sounds
Of your gentle voice
The warming laughter
The songs of simple faith

This tapestry has reached its end
The story found its fading finale
Yet we will hold the tale aloft
On the flood of our hearts
Immortal in the onrushing dreams

Drifting into Dream Dimensions

Field of vision blurred in the soft light
Twinkling in faint hues of red and green
Sharpening the edges of a towering Fir
Commanding this cozy living room
With the heady scent of northern pine
While a log slowly succumbs to flame
And emanates a calming warmth
On these icy December nights
With our jovial celebrations winding down
Towards a quiet hibernation sleep
In the arms of the longest Winter
Dreaming of fabled Spring

Something That Smells Like Freedom

We danced
We dreamed
We decided it was worth taking a chance on being alive
We never stopped to ask for directions
We figured it would all make sense once the merry-go-round stopped moving
We asked for just one more
cause there's always room for jello
We thought a tattoo really was the best memento
We never let anyone tell us there was something beyond our ability
We never gave up on each other
We laughed
We cried
We smiled cause we always forgot the last line

Flames aren't Meant for Bathing

We never really stop to contemplate light
Or consider the implications of breathing
As an undeniable necessity to existence

We linger in the imaginary grip of darkness
Captured by the vanity of blind anxiety
And the irrational weight of fear

We never speak of these soul confusions
Choosing willful self-immolation
Over admission of inadequacy

We'd rather burn in our own private hell
Then ever dare ask for help from heaven

...or from anyone at all really...

Knowing the Words doesn't Make it Your Song

I thought to lose myself in her eyes
And in the endless celestial melody
Spread across the shrinking distance
Between longing and satisfaction
Buried beyond our feigned direction

I chased the ephemera of your memory
Trying to recapture shadows of ghosts
And a feeling long disappeared
That no amount of passing lust could ever satiate

Chasing Shrinking Rainbows at Sundown

Emerald

That was the color that glittered in your reflection
As it danced in the hidden pool
Nestled within a shrouded grove
Where we used to play as children

Laughter

A sound so joyfully wonderful
Hinting at the mirth and merriment
We hoped would carry on
Cradling our innocence
Like a long-forgotten keepsake

Silence

The kind you wish was comfortable
Full of questions and riddles
With no sense of comprehension
And leaves nothing for certainty
Except a growing sense of loathing
For these unbidden enigmas

<u>Existential Terror wasn't Part of the Deal</u>

What was it about the absence of starlight
That brought on such unshakeable dread?
More than just the ambient light pollution
Or the suffocating industrial fog
There was simply no illumination left

No light rays streaking across galaxies
To sparkle in the evening indigo overhead

No glittering dust incinerating on entry
Fueling adolescent wishes

The interstellar firebrands slowly vanished
Constellations erased from their tapestries
And it felt like the universal battery
Was fading to nothing

In that moment
We learned exactly how small we truly are

Swallowing Swords in E Minor

Epiphany often arrives somewhat late
In an inattentive fashion
Punctuated in fits and bursts of eureka
Stabbing through our encrusted melancholia

We'd like to believe all these revelations
Result from careful reconstructions
And soulful meditations
More than these brilliant accidents
That seem to define our entwined existence

Knowledge gained and wisdom earned
Are never lost for merit
Despite their stubborn hindsight application
Ignorance is hardly bliss
Amid all this self-discovery

Having all the words doesn't automatically
Loosen the tongue or stifle anxieties
And yet I have unleashed crimson rivers
In pursuit of this love
With an ocean more awaiting
Should the need arise
And these salty scars are war stories
Tattooed testament of my devotion

It was always you
I have no other love to speak of
No other heart that beats in this rhythm
Just slightly out of key

If You See Alice, Tell Her She's Late

I tumbled down the rabbit hole
And out into the unknowing ether
In the hope of finding something
Magical in the wilderness beyond

Simple daydream doldrums
Give birth to middle-age desperation
Spent chasing rose tinted nostalgia
And a myth of better yesterdays

I'm just the lonely phantom
Of a forgotten man of tomorrow
Left to haunt this skeleton
Hanging in your wonderland

Hummingbird Heartbeats

Windswept and carried away
Alight in a flight of fancy
Born in the smoldering ashes
Of a phoenix daydream
And a million 'what-ifs'
That tickle fraying nerves
Bent beyond the edge of possibility

This Would Be a Good Moment for Forever

The first shafts of sunlight
Splintered the cold gray horizon
In arcing streaks of gold
Unveiling renewed promises
At the awakening of dawn

I listen to the gentle rhythm of your breathing
Steady and content beside me
And I wonder what dreams may dance
Inside such fitful slumber

Only a little longer yet
'til this rest meets an end
And the ambient silence shatters
Pierced through by the alarm bell din

Film at Eleven

Left myself wide open
Exposed to the hungry inquiries
Of a world ever unsatisfied
Seeking the next outstretched soul
To eviscerate and devour

There was no miscalculation made
No misguided naivete
More akin to a desperation ploy
And some softcore marketing fad

Mr. DeMille…
I'm ready for my close-up

Lamented Plateau Visions

The desert beckons in the birth of Spring
Whispering ancient verses on the western wind
Rolling through canyon crevices and carvings
That paint a forgotten history
Bleached and tattooed beneath the alien sun
In such an unforgiving land

We did not break under the grim weight
Of your manifest destiny obsession
Nor did we disappear
Into this sterile homogenization
You cling to as progressive achievement
At imagination's expense

Our blood still stains the rock and sand
Our song still howls with the moonlight
We are the inextinguishable spirit
Indigenous and free

Guided Tours of Topeka

Coral tinted lenses
Shade ocular senses
And paint perception
In pleasant hue refractions
That color newfound adulation
Within nostalgic permutations
To avoid unwanted inquiries
Into the state of mental faculties

Just sing along my dear
And pay no attention
To the wizard's smoke and mirrors

NEDERLAND 2½ CENT

LEIDEN 10.2.11.8-9 N

BRIEFKAART

LEIDEN 8-9 N

AAN den Weledelgeb. Heer

J. F. Hulk

Teyler's Stichting

Damstraat

Haarlem

A.16

HAARLEM 7 10.2.11.11-12 N

Naam en Adres des Afzenders

(Desverkiezende in te vullen).

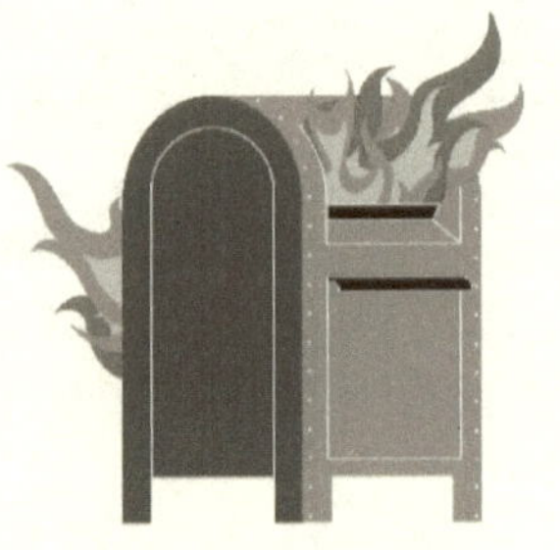

Wallflowers Don't Take Center Stage

I picked the perfect time
To crash your party scene
By which of course I mean
I was never quite invited
Nor welcome in such idyllic fantasies
So carefully constructed
To meet those exacting bourgeoisie dreams

But hey, there's always one, right?
One unlucky soul caught out unawares
Left to fumble through invented niceties
And wonder what exactly is the point
Of all these boring little routines
Meant to impress this self-styled royalty

I watch it all unfold in utter bemusement
Hoarding cheap hors d'oeurves
And watered-down cocktails
While you entertain advances
From lecherous socialites
You shun in daylight circles

Being an invisible man is much preferred
To all this pomp and circumstance
And yet I somehow seem to wish
Just once
That you might deign to ask me in

Dreaming Under Tables

The sound of ants marching
Echoed through the corridor
And gave way to errant thoughts
Of crawling destinies
Shuffling out of mind
Out of reach
Evaporating in the swollen breach
Left to drift along untethered
Listening to the monotone meandering
Morse code conversations
Hidden in the sounds of ants marching
That echoes through the corridor…

Brain Chemistry Overdrive

I've told myself so many different accounts
Of the unfolding events
And painted a thousand variations
Of this still life representation
That came to overshadow
The reality stretched between our souls
Until it was simply impossible to remember
The undeniable truth we sought out in the beginning
When we were young and so blissfully ignorant
Of all these painful reveries
Among the hollow sepulchers
Of the easily amused and terminally bored
That it's not hard to imagine the confusion
We found ourselves wading into
And yet somehow we still thought
To remain unchanged and undeterred
Until the morning we woke up unrecognizable
And wondering if there was any way back
To the golden shore divine

Ghosts Headed West

Faded blue notes still float in the desert
Drifting on the howling summer wind
That recalls the free roaming jazz poetry
Hitchhiking with the ghost of the Beats
Along an abandoned highway winding west
Toward a disappearing sun
And the promise of a welcoming night

Nicknames and Favorite Scents

A simple elegance often overstated
Woven within silken petals ever in bloom
And bound up in the sweetest cliché
Dangling in an awkward offering
And pressed between pages unread

Games of Fools and Lovers

I always wondered if you found it
That earnest observation
Framed within a hidden question
Scrawled in haphazard script
Tucked away inside vellum pages
Of a novel long forgotten

Hanging on the Wings of Your Intention

Awakening to a western sunrise
Cresting the horizon of alien skies
That illuminates a digital Babylon
Stretching out extraplanetary
Recalling an overactive imagination
Filtered through a scanner darkly
And recognizing a stranger in a strange land
Whispering how the moon is a harsh mistress
While seeking comfort in the icy grip
Of the left hand of darkness
While attempting to win the affections
Of a princess of Mars
Who is far too modest to dream
Of a foregone conclusion
Or dare hope to adequately receive
The once and future king

Weekend Insomniac Parade

Drifting down forgotten alleys
Dirty arteries outlined in grime
Carrying urban lifeblood
Through an industrial heart
Pumping sludge and ash
To feed the undying machine
That never rests within
A city that never seems to sleep

Playing with Perception

Pale shadows populate shallow daydreams
Passing unbidden through idle wanderlust
Pretending to ponder the scope of existence
Preferring the quiet unsung ambivalence

Monuments Gloriously Mismanaged

The spires beckoned
Stabbing backwards
Sculpted by careful eons
And the fingers of a thunderstorm
Painting desert sandstone
With a wide brush of flash flood
And a flourish of lightning
Signaling our rapid descent
In the shadowed valley undead

Horizons and Other Faded Dreams

Lost in thought
Floating between the color and the shape
Rising on rolling summer tides
And breathing in the salted breeze
Forever searching for the moment
When the ocean meets the sky

All the Live Long Day

Westbound on Pacific Rail
Hitching a boxcar ride
With the dustbowl ghosts
Still dreaming of an America
Dead in the dusk
Back beyond the crash of '29

Total Recall Wasn't in the Cards

The details have gotten rather hazy
In the wake of all the years long past
And I can't quite bring to mind
A remembrance of our design
A resemblance of our direction
Or a star we thought to wish upon

Bayou Battle Hymn

We saw the fog rolling in slowly
Obscuring the marshy dwellings
Decrepit and uninhabited
Sheathed in misty gray
And molding decay
Wondering if it's invasion
Or surrender
To the creeping reclamation
Of this slaughter swamp unbound

Technomancer in Loathing

I thought it was something like breathing
But altogether different
In this digital recreation
Balanced on a binary foundation
Driving an addiction for identical simulation
That pulls every piece into an ideal creation
With me at the absolute center of existence
With every notion of stepping back into actual reality
Shouted down by the cold comfort of ones and zeroes
Bent to my will in a web of imagined safety
Far from the unwelcome truth and pain
Of my lackluster significance
And any number of other lies
I choose to believe and run from
In this self-induced waking coma

Simple Instruments

They're simple instruments
Wood and nails
Implements of construction
Exclamations of death
Bent on the whim of perspective
Tools of a father's trade
Set aside for the Father's purpose
Revisited in another's grip
Wood and nails
Fashioned in an execution march

Wood and Nails
Stone and Steel
An empty tomb
A Risen King

...and in Cursive No Less...

Realization arrives in static waves
Cresting the surface of the shallows
We never seemed to move beyond
Dulled in the honeyed promises
Dangling in the hangman's snare
Laced with a malformed hope
And the illusion of change

I'm tired of writing love letters
To the ghost of who we used to be

Navigating the Open Seas of Confusion Between Us

I think there was maybe a kind of misunderstanding
Unearthed in between the friendship
And the anticipation of something
Beyond the bounds of platonic
And I'm starting to feel a bit less cognizant
Of the spoken motives that pass for acceptable rationale
Within the course of an echoing diatribe
Spilling from lips that never seem to close
And a sound meant to condition the nature of violence
We pretend to have no taste for
But crave like the sweetest ambrosia nectar

The wheels start to turn
Giving way to eureka shouts
And troubled epiphanies
Revealing a certain misunderstanding
That hangs between the friendship and the fear

I'm not Saying I'm Shakespeare but...

We want to believe that our words
Reveal a sweeping inspiration
That sparks the unfolding imagination
Of the increasingly global persuasion
That captures this gasping frustration
Eliminated by intellectual illumination

...and perhaps they are...

But if we're being honest here
This is typically where the guts are spilled
The tears are shed
And we perform a half-assed exorcism
On the collective demons in our heads

Comfort Doesn't Equal Healthy

I tried to delineate these thoughts
That scream for undivided attention
Pounding in the shrinking pulse
Palpitated through a deadly rhythm
Telegraphed by a military tattoo
Calling forth the endless march
Of neurotic overthought opinions

I tried but they never quite make sense
In the realm of rationality
Never quite connect outside the bounds of disarray
Or the comfort of carnality

You're not a Dead Sparkler, You're an Eternal Flame

The mirror has been dark for so long
That I worry all that's ever seen
Is the shadowed reflection
Of this passing trouble
That clings with icy talons
In a grip that speaks to desperation
Rather than the kind of control
It would have the world believe it possesses
Over this tentative heart thundering in my chest
In the heat of exhilaration
That begs for a chance to be seen

Open your eyes
And look past that tainted mirror
To see the light and hope that burns so bright
It could never be contained
In the meager vessels we tend to offer
In adulation and supplication on hallowed ground
Don't be afraid to let it consume you
And give rise to the undying flame
You were always meant to be

You're not the Martyr You Made Yourself Out to Be

There might have been a time
When I thought all this bleeding
Both literal and figurative
Was the highest expression of love
I might possess for you
And yet I find the measure wanting
Falling short of my potential
In the blinding realization
That the pain is not the ideation
Or anything more than a fleeting emotion

No, the proof is in the will to choose
And the sacrificial follow through
Accepting that true growth only occurs
In our mutually scarred unity
And the warmth of the healing light

Dream Language and Vision Starter Packs

There was a dream we once shared
A tiny spark glowing in the ether
It called out in the midst of our waking slumber
Trying to rouse us from the stupor
we let consume our very existence
But it feels like nothing more than a distant memory
only vaguely imagined
Like the melody from a lullaby
that you recall but can't place
The one you seem to hum to yourself
whenever the moment is free
The words dance on the tip of your tongue
yet never come
Not unlike the way I'm numb every time you pass by
And I remember a dream we once shared…

Sunglasses and Summer Boys

Sheets of foam slide along the sand
Rushing in to cover tiny toes
That scramble back up the shore
Children happily giggling in escape
Watching the waves slip back to sea
Repeating until the thrill subsides
And the sun soars against the azure
Brilliant and cloudless
Baking in the summer sauna

I remember all those afternoons
Lazy recollections in the twilight
Though I no longer run
Preferring now the swirling cool
That splashes over tired feet
Tasting the salty kisses
Floating on the gentle breeze
Basking in the easy promise
Of another holiday routine

<u>Falling had Nothing to do with It</u>

I've been living with your ghost
Since long before you were gone
And even when I didn't mind the haunting
I still missed the totality of your presence
And can't deny my own aimless drifting
Or recognize the slowly dying flame

It's never been about assigning blame
We both know our own culpability
Share an equally valid accusation
Of believing the emotional hype
That fuels the 'love' masquerade
That drowned us in our self-service

We forgot that our feelings are crooked
Speaking easily digested falsehoods
Love is a deliberate choice
Made even in the absence of attraction
Outside the whim of desire
One we neglected well before the end

Needles, Spoons, and Other Weapons of Self-Destruction

A simple choice in the beginning
Almost innocent in scope
And it just felt so good to be high
To chase that euphoric feeling
'til the candles burnt down to stubs
And I couldn't remember my own name
Just one more line
One more pill
One more fix
Chasing the dragon into the dark
At the expense of everyone
The cost of everything
Giving little thought to the pain
Or the burning bridges
But I can see the tracks of tears
On my mother's face
And hear her lament in the twilight
That rose to a wailing by morning
When the dragon finally won

It was the End and I Felt Fine

...and if the last star fell from the sky tonight
Burning a trail against the midnight indigo
I'd chase those dying embers
Until their light was but a memory
And our time a soulful song
On some long-forgotten radio...

Concertos and Requiems we Thought to Memorize

The pendulum swings
Bound by an unseen rhythm
And an indecipherable time signature
That leaves us with only questions
And a metronome that can't find the pace
In a symphony we still hope to follow
Though the parts we thought to learn
Are lost in an unfamiliar harmony
Descending to a minor key better left unsung

We cling to the sweetest melody
The one we sang that very first time
We knew the touch of the truest love
And know even further still
That it warms us even now
In the midst of an unknown movement
And a shortage of direction
From our most trusted conductor
Who completely embodies the song

Chess Pieces Playing Checkers

I spent all those nights bleeding out
In what I thought to be a shining ideal
That only served to mask the wounds
I suffered at the hands of visionaries
That only had utility in mind
And were quick to discard the refuse
Once we outlived our purpose
A voluntary casualty in the ascent
Of the cult of personality

I think I must be dreaming now
This can't really be the end
Everything went white
Such a disappointing cliché

If You were More Symbiotic Maybe We Could Talk...

This might be quite the surprise
But I've never settled into something
That I one day planned to eradicate
Like an unfortunate plague

"Having a great time with you
Can't wait to survey the eventual wreckage
And one day burn away
Every trace of our entanglement"

Those aren't the kind of thoughts
That frame my initial outlook
On what this might become

But I suppose if they were obvious
These parasites that roam free
Would find the road more difficult
And willing hosts a bit scarce

Still, this fire was not my first choice
But you kept handing me matches
And I'll be damned if more than ashes
Remain come morning

Light Everlasting

We wander in these lazy moments
The ones that seem to float aloft
Dancing on the rising summer breeze
Wondering if we're still sleeping
Dreaming through an afterlife
Or awake in the faintest hint of calm
And trying to ignore a coming storm
The kind that breeds uncertainty
And hold the door for anxiety

Right now it's peaceful
Quiet settling in the hills
And we're choosing to believe
All will be well
That this hope is undying
And our true home
Is cresting the horizon

<u>Deafened in the Moment</u>

The sound is missing
Lost in a haze of terror that descended
Shattering what should've been an ordinary Saturday
One full of laughter and chatter
Frantic rush for school supplies
Casual dates and drinks to celebrate
But instead found an armored appetizer
And a barrage of bullets doused in hatred

Everyone is running
Faces painted in horror
Screaming but the sound is missing
I can feel it tearing from my throat
But there's nothing
Nothing

Enraptured is an Understatement

We talk about the experience
The moments we spent entangled
Breathing in unison
Recalling the replay like distant memory
But the taste of you has never vanished
And your scent still colors my senses
Entertaining an ecstatic kaleidoscope
Wrapped within a fever dream

…where we talk about the experience
And the endless moments spent entangled

Or Am I Too Numb to Care?

I laid myself down
Spread out on the verdant lawn
Bathing in the golden light
Blazing in the dying summer heat
Soaking in the searing warmth
Amid internal reflections
On the state of soul and spirit
And I'm not sure exactly
Just what that really means
But there's a song in the distance
A softly mumbled lullaby
And I'm too comfortable to notice
The ravenous reptile
Slowly swallowing me whole

Secret Melodies in the Key of Me

We aspire to grand narratives
Hung like constellations
Spread out among virgin galaxies
Hidden beyond the furthest reaches
That carry on a coveted legacy

We crave remembrance
Elusive and enigmatic
A phantom orchid rarely in bloom
That we hunt relentlessly
Leaving blood and ink currency
Staining parchment pages
And washed out photographs
Obscured artifacts
Scattered throughout our destiny
Littered echoes half begotten
Dreamt aloud in déjà vu

Solemn September Skyline

I remember the quiet hum
Florescent tubes glowing so ordinary
Like any other Tuesday in the store
And then the phone started ringing

"did you hear?!"
"Turn on the news!"

The sights that followed
Left us cold and numb
And I can still see the collapse
Hear the shock and disbelief
Watched true heroes spring to life

18 years behind us
A fractured skyline
Still reminding
Of a dreadful mid-September past

Burning the Candles Alone

There's no shortage of poignant lines
And clever rhymes
No end to the wordplay wizardry
Inhabiting this practiced pen
Or the de Bergerac inspiration
Whispered in the shadowed glen

Never worried much about the pages
Being filled or read
More so having all these perfect words
And no one to say them to

Exit Strategies for Unneeded Labels

Awakened in the aftermath
Rising unshackled from our past
In the light of redemptive grace
Breathing in life
Maybe the first time in decades
Wondering at the newfound clarity
Surveying monuments to memories
That populate this odd menagerie
And illuminate these storied pages
Bringing purpose to the pain
A new path to follow
A new fire to burn

Stolen Moons and Comet Constellations

Crawling across the cosmic veil
Investigating interstellar secrets
Hidden deep within anachronous galaxies
Lost to the pulse of history
Spread out among the distant nebulae
Wondering what lies beneath
The phantom atmosphere
What undiscovered geography
Is waiting to be known
At the awakening of alien suns
In the coastal skies

We are the last explorers in flight
Challenging the cresting event horizon
And the enveloping chill of the void

Better Dreams on the Horizon

Walking the edge of a precipice
A kind of dance you find familiar
Testing the limits of the unknown
And knowing you're called out beyond
Far from the comfortable safety
Most cling to for reassurance
Called to let go of things hoped for
And trust that what's received
Will far outshine the imagined sheen
Of these temporary baubles

Another year has spun the wheel
One more trip around the sun
And the pages in this diary are open
Alive and eagerly anticipating
The next thrilling adventure abroad

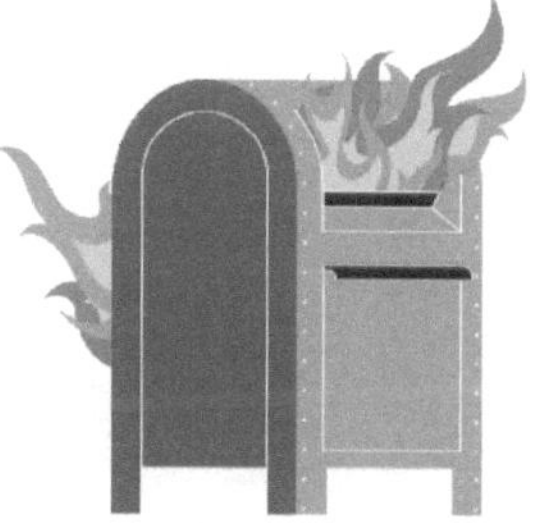

More Titles Available from David Greshel and Neon Sunrise Publishing:

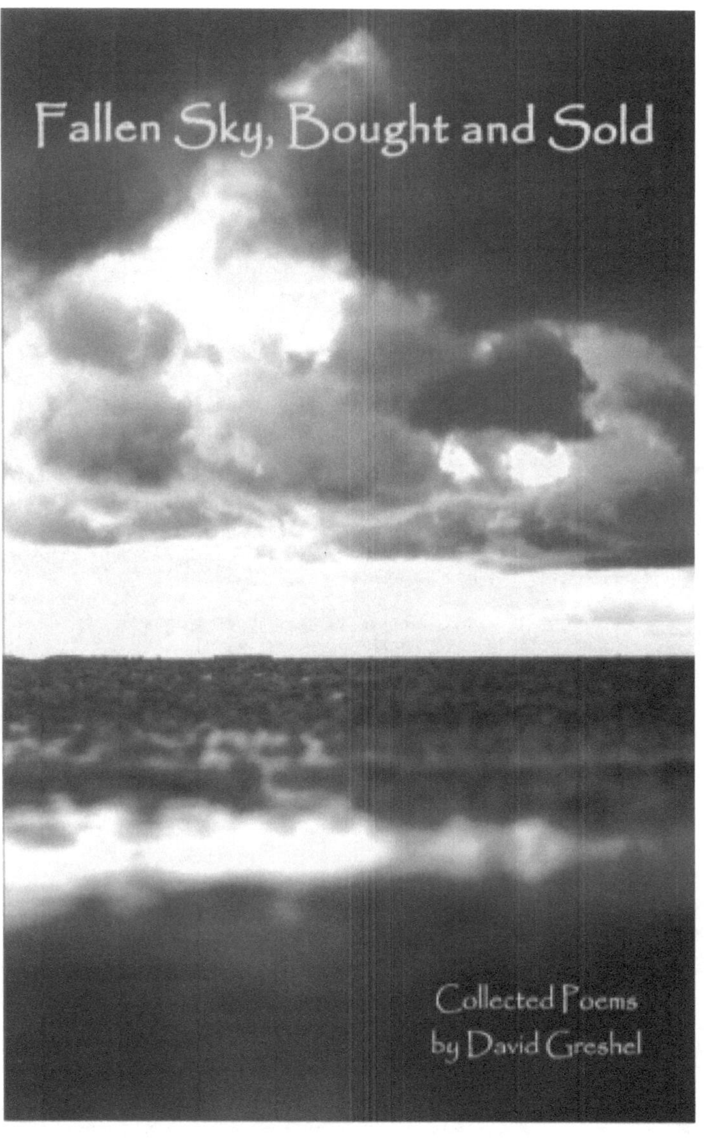

NOMADS, PILGRIMS, TROUBADOURS

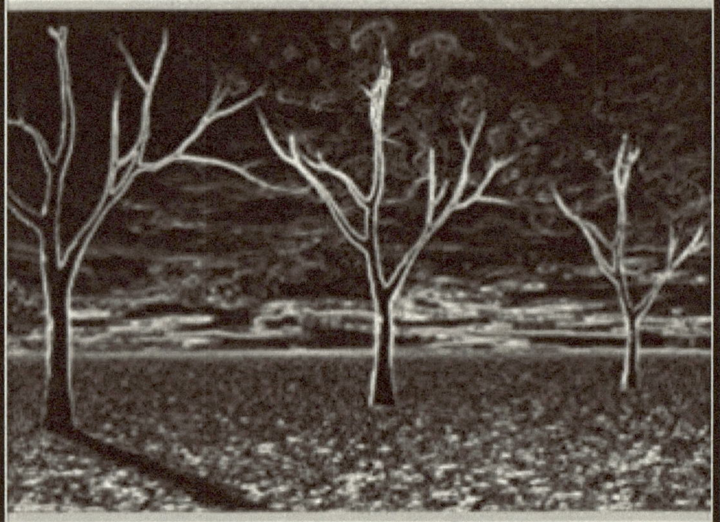

DAVID GRESHEL

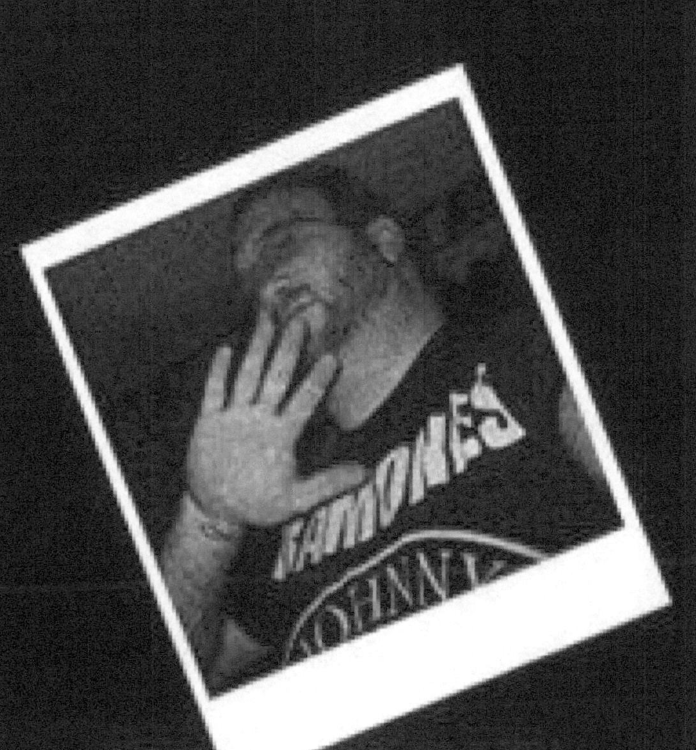

WINDOWS INTO THE PAST FOR THE CAMERA SHY

DAVID GRESHEL

About the Author/Contact Info

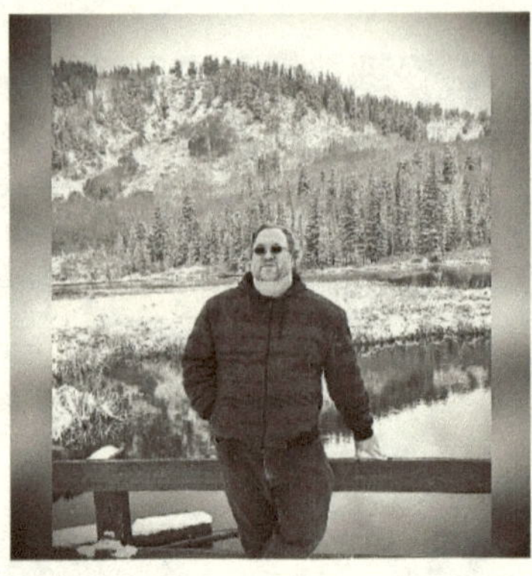

David Greshel is a Mississippi-born, Florida-bred author and poet with a penchant for music, movies, and all things pop culture. Never one to shy away from self-reflection and evaluation, he channels it all into his writing with the results you now see before you.

David currently resides in Palm Bay Florida and can often be found at live music events when not working, writing, or spending time with friends and family.

This is his fourth collection of poetry. His first three collections - Windows into the Past for the Camera Shy, Nomads, Pilgrims, Troubadours, and Fallen Sky, Bought and Sold - are also available everywhere.

Connect with David:

Email: dgreshel217@gmail.com
Facebook: facebook.com/david.greshel
Instagram: @electricinfamy
Twitter: @electricpoet217
Website: www.neonsunrisebooks.com

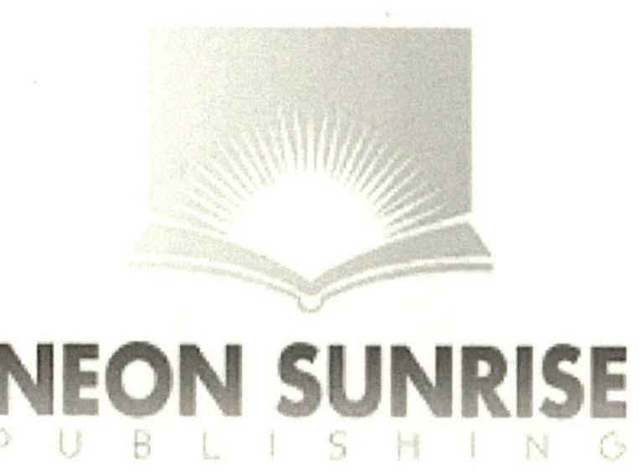

Neon Sunrise Publishing is focused on helping independent creators realize their dreams of seeing their books in print. We're driven by a DIY spirit and a desire to provide options and resources to help developing talent succeed in sharing their voice with the world.

To keep up with all of our latest news and releases, be sure to join our mailing list and connect with us online!

Email: neonsunrisepub@gmail.com
Facebook: facebook.com/neonsunrisepub
Instagram: @neonsunrisepub
Twitter: @neonsunrisepub
Website: www.neonsunrisepublishing.com

www.ingramcontent.com/pod-product-compliance
Lightning Source LLC
LaVergne TN
LVHW050959080826
845145LV00009B/2358
* 9 7 8 1 7 3 5 7 3 6 0 1 3 *